What Is a Bank?

BY DANA MEACHEN RAU

READING CONSULTANT: SUSAN NATIONS, M.ED., AUTHOR/LITERACY COACH/CONSULTANT

WR WEEKLY READER
EARLY LEARNING LIBRARY

Please visit our web site at: www.earlyliteracy.cc
For a free color catalog describing Weekly Reader® Early Learning Library's list
of high-quality books, call 1-877-445-5824 (USA) or 1-800-387-3178 (Canada).
Weekly Reader® Early Learning Library's fax: (414) 336-0164.

Library of Congress Cataloging-in-Publication Data

Rau, Dana Meachen, 1971–
    What is a bank? / by Dana Meachen Rau.
      p. cm. — (Money and banks)
    Includes bibliographical references and index.
    ISBN 0-8368-4873-X (lib. bdg.)
    ISBN 0-8368-4880-2 (softcover)
    1. Banks and banking—Juvenile literature. I. Title. II. Series.
  HG1609.R38   2005
  332.1—dc22   2005042209

This edition first published in 2006 by
Weekly Reader® Early Learning Library
A Member of the WRC Media Family of Companies
330 West Olive Street, Suite 100
Milwaukee, WI 53212 USA

Editor: Barbara Kiely Miller
Art direction: Tammy West
Cover design and page layout: Dave Kowalski
Picture research: Diane Laska-Swanke

Picture credits: Cover, title, pp. 4, 5, 6, 7, 9, 10, 11, 13, 15, 16, 17, 18, 19 Gregg Andersen;
p. 8 Diane Laska-Swanke

Printed in the United States of America

1 2 3 4 5 6 7 8 9 09 08 07 06 05

Table of Contents

Chapter ① A Big Piggy Bank

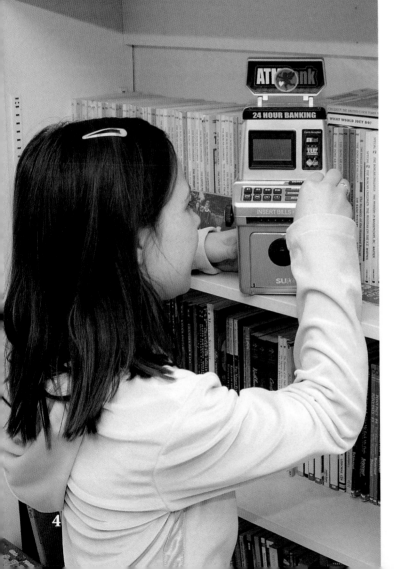

Where do you keep your money? You might have a small bank in your room. Some banks are shaped like animals. Some have places for each kind of coin.

Many children save their money at home in small banks.

4

Most towns and cities have one or more banks.

One type of bank would not fit in your room. **Bank** is also the name for a building that holds money. It is like a giant piggy bank.

You may save so much money that the bank in your room is full. Then you and a parent can open a savings account at a bank in your town or city. This bank is a safe place to keep your money.

All the members of your family can keep their money in the bank.

A teller will help you open a savings account. The **teller** is the person behind the counter at the bank. Your account will have both your name and your parent's name on it. Now you can put money into your account at the bank.

A teller can answer all of your questions about saving your money at the bank.

7

A **deposit** is the money you put into your account. You keep track of the money in your account in a **bankbook**. When you deposit money into your account, you or the teller will add the amount to your bankbook.

A bankbook is small and easy to carry.

A **withdrawal** is money that is taken out of the bank. Your parent is the only person who can take money out of your account. The teller gives you and your parent the money you need. Then you or the teller subtracts the amount from your bankbook.

Your parent must help you take money out of your bank account when you need it.

9

People do not need to go to a bank teller to make a withdrawal. Sometimes, they do not have time to go to the bank. They can use ATM machines to get money quickly. An ATM machine is sometimes called an "Automatic Teller Machine."

ATMs are a fast and easy way to get money. You might see ATMs in the grocery store, at the mall, or even at an amusement park.

A person puts an ATM card into a slot on the machine. Then he or she types in a special number code and the amount of money to take out, or **withdraw**. The money, a receipt, and the ATM card come out of the machine.

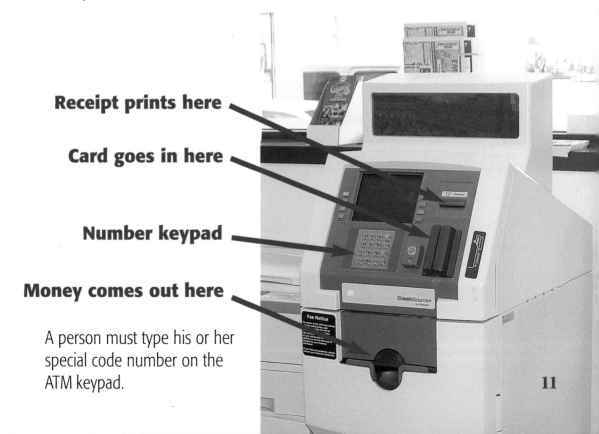

Receipt prints here

Card goes in here

Number keypad

Money comes out here

A person must type his or her special code number on the ATM keypad.

11

The bank does not keep all the money you put into your account. It uses your money to help other people. The bank puts a little extra money in your account every month to thank you for letting them use your savings. This extra money is called **interest**.

	SAVINGS REGISTER						
DATE	DESCRIPTION OF TRANSACTION	WITHDRAWAL		DEPOSITS & INTEREST	BAL. BR'T F'R'D	✓	
					AMOUNT OF TRANSACTION		
					BALANCE		
					AMOUNT OF TRANSACTION		
					BALANCE		
					AMOUNT OF TRANSACTION		
					BALANCE		
					AMOUNT OF TRANSACTION		
					BALANCE		
					AMOUNT OF TRANSACTION		
					BALANCE		

A bankbook has places to write down the interest the bank pays you.

					AMOUNT OF TRANSACTION		
					BALANCE		
					AMOUNT OF TRANSACTION		
					BALANCE		
					AMOUNT OF TRANSACTION		
					BALANCE		
					AMOUNT OF TRANSACTION		
					BALANCE		
					AMOUNT OF TRANSACTION		
					BALANCE		
					AMOUNT OF TRANSACTION		
					BALANCE		

PLEASE RECORD EACH TRANSACTION

Sometimes adults want to buy something that costs a lot of money. They might not have enough money in the bank. The bank will lend them the money they need. This money is called a **loan**.

Adults must sign papers before a bank will give them a loan.

When you borrow a book from the library, you have to bring it back. A bank works this way, too. When a bank lends customers money, the customers must pay the money back. The customers must also pay the bank interest for letting them borrow the money.

The interest on a loan can be a big part of the loan payment.

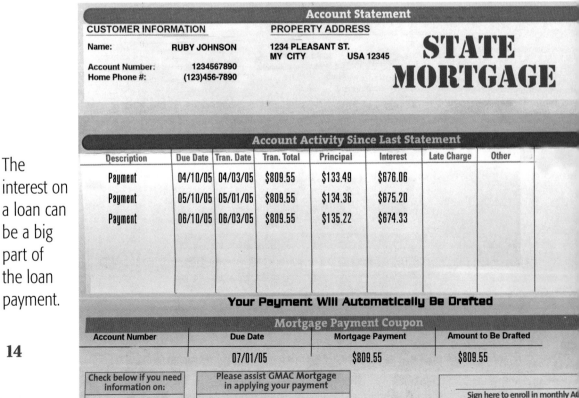

Account Statement

CUSTOMER INFORMATION		PROPERTY ADDRESS	
Name:	RUBY JOHNSON	1234 PLEASANT ST.	
		MY CITY	USA 12345
Account Number:	1234567890		
Home Phone #:	(123)456-7890		

STATE MORTGAGE

Account Activity Since Last Statement

Description	Due Date	Tran. Date	Tran. Total	Principal	Interest	Late Charge	Other
Payment	04/10/05	04/03/05	$809.55	$133.49	$676.06		
Payment	05/10/05	05/01/05	$809.55	$134.36	$675.20		
Payment	06/10/05	06/03/05	$809.55	$135.22	$674.33		

Your Payment Will Automatically Be Drafted

Mortgage Payment Coupon

Account Number	Due Date	Mortgage Payment	Amount to Be Drafted
	07/01/05	$809.55	$809.55

Check below if you need information on:	Please assist GMAC Mortgage in applying your payment	Sign here to enroll in monthly AC

Adults might borrow money to buy a house. They usually have thirty years to pay the money back. Other types of loans need to be paid back much quicker. Adults must pay back a loan for a car in only about three or four years. The sooner they pay back the money, the less interest they have to pay.

Banks help families by giving them loans to buy their own homes.

15

The bank keeps money in a vault. A **vault** is a room with a thick, locked door. Only people working at the bank can get into the vault.

The door to a bank vault is made of thick metal.

16

Some banks also have safe-deposit boxes. **Safe-deposit boxes** look like a wall of locked drawers in different sizes. They are like small vaults for customers to use.

Bank customers can pick a large safe-deposit box, a small box, or a medium-sized one.

Each safe-deposit box has two keyholes. The customer keeps one key. The bank keeps the other key. Both keys are needed to open a safe-deposit box. People put things in safe-deposit boxes that they do not want to lose. They might keep important papers or jewelry in their safe-deposit boxes.

Each safe-deposit box is locked tight and needs two keys to open it.

Is there a toy you want to buy? Is it time to buy a birthday present for a friend? You can ask your parent to take you to the bank and take money out of your account. The money you put into a bank is always there when you need it.

The money you keep in a bank will earn extra money for you to spend later.

19

Learn how to keep track of your savings account in a bankbook. Make a copy of page 21 or use a piece of paper. Then add and subtract the numbers below to find out what the total in this bank account, or its **balance**, would be at the end of one year.

Date	Description of Transaction
January 10	Start account
February 5	Buy a new toy
June 30	Interest from the bank
July 21	Money from chores
September 30	Buy school supplies
December 16	Gift from Grandma
December 31	Interest from the bank

	Withdrawal	Deposit	Balance
		$25.00	$25.00
	$1.00		
		$0.50	
		$5.00	
	$2.00		
		$3.00	
		$0.60	

The correct answer is on page 23.

Glossary

bankbook – a small book that shows the money put into and taken out of a bank account

deposit – (n) an amount of money added to a bank account; (v) to put money into a bank account

interest – money that is paid or charged for the use of borrowed money

lend – to give someone money that must be repaid

receipt – a written slip of paper that shows how much money was put into or taken out of a bank account

savings account – an account at a bank on which interest is paid

teller – the person who works behind the counter at a bank

vault – a locked room in a bank where money is kept

withdrawal – an amount of money taken out of a bank account

For More Information

Books

Bank Tellers. Community Workers (series). Cynthia Klingel and Robert B. Noyed (Compass Point Books)

Money. Mighty Math (series). Sara Pistoia (Child's World)

Round and Round the Money Goes: What Money Is and How We Use It. Discovery Readers (series). Melvin Berger (Ideals Publications)

Web Sites

The Mint: How Banks Work
www.themint.org/saving/howbankswork.php
Information about saving money at a bank

Kids Bank.com
www.kidsbank.com
Learn about saving money and how a bank works.

Index

About the Author

Dana Meachen Rau is an author, editor, and illustrator. She has written more than one hundred books for children, including nonfiction, early readers, and historical fiction. She lives with her family in Burlington, Connecticut.